ELEMENTS OF *Wri*

PORTFOLIO ASSESSMENT

TEACHING NOTES AND MODEL FORMS

▶ **First Course**

HOLT, RINEHART AND WINSTON

Harcourt Brace & Company

Austin • *New York* • *Orlando* • *Atlanta* • *San Francisco* • *Boston* • *Dallas* • *Toronto* • *London*

Staff Credits

Associate Director: Mescal Evler

Managing Editor: Steve Welch

Project Editors: Susan Sims Britt, Susan Lynch

Editorial Staff: *Editors,* Jonathan David Carson, Adrienne Greer; *Copy Editors,* Joseph S. Schofield IV, Atietie O. Tonwe; *Coordinators,* Susan G. Alexander, Amanda F. Beard, Rebecca Bennett, Wendy Langabeer, Marie Hoffman Price; *Support,* Ruth A. Hooker, Kelly Keeley, Margaret Sanchez, Pat Stover

Design: Christine Schueler

Editorial Permissions: Janet Harrington

Production Coordinator: Rosa Mayo Degollado

Electronic Publishing Supervisor: Barbara Hudgens

Electronic Publishing Staff: Heather Jernt, *Project Coordinator*
JoAnn Brown, David Hernandez, Rina May Ouellette, Charlie Taliaferro, Ethan Thompson

Contributing Writers

Judith Austin-Mills
Bill Martin
Matthew H. Pangborn
Raymond Teague

Printed in the United States of America

ISBN 0-03-051148-8

1 2 3 4 5 085 00 99 98 97

Contents

To the Teacher

The teacher support provided by the *Annotated Teacher's Edition* is further reinforced by the *Teaching Resources*.

The *Teaching Resources* have been designed to help you in your classroom—where the demands on your time and energy are great—to deal with each student as an individual.

This booklet, *Portfolio Assessment,* contains a portfolio of materials that you may use to develop your own system of portfolio assessment. It provides a brief overview of some portfolio assessment options and a collection of forms and checklists that you and students may use or adapt for evaluating student work and assessing progress in reading, writing, speaking, listening, and viewing.

Portfolio Assessment is the seventh in a series of eight booklets comprising the *Teaching Resources.*

- *Practicing the Writing Process*
- *Strategies for Writing*
- *Word Choice and Sentence Style*
- *Language Skills Practice and Assessment*
- *Academic and Workplace Skills*
- *Holistic Scoring: Prompts and Models*
- **Portfolio Assessment**
- *Practice for Assessment in Reading, Vocabulary, and Spelling*

Portfolio Assessment

This section of the *Teaching Resources* provides you with a portfolio of materials that you may use to assess student work and evaluate progress. The evaluation sheets, checklists, and tests are appropriate for inclusion in student portfolios, or they may be used independently of portfolio assessment.

PORTFOLIO ASSESSMENT

The *Elements of Writing* program is designed to allow teachers flexibility in creating, maintaining, and evaluating student portfolios. The portfolio forms included in this booklet are not only prompts and guides to help your students think critically about the work they are collecting, but also are tools to evaluate and organize portfolio contents. These forms will help you establish basic records of language activity and provide information on the language background that students bring to class. They also will help in goal setting for you and your students.

If you are interested in a portfolio approach to assessment, you many want to consider one of the following options.

The Basic Portfolio. Many teachers prefer a portfolio that is limited to a few samples of a student's writing, perhaps a diagnostic essay and four to six finished essays representing the student's best efforts over the course of the academic year. Ordinarily, the teacher and the student collaborate to make the selections, perhaps choosing a piece every six to nine weeks of the school year.

The portfolio is evaluated two to four times during the academic year. Usually the teacher and the student meet together to assess the portfolio. They discuss what criteria the portfolio should meet, and they consider how well the student's work meets the criteria. Both students and teachers find it helpful to have a list of the criteria clipped to the portfolio.

If the portfolios are being used to assess a writing program rather than the progress of individual students, a random sampling of portfolios should provide reliable information regarding the program's achievements.

The Mastery Portfolio. Some teachers prefer to maintain portfolios that contain student responses to specific prompts designed to test student mastery of a particular objective—writing for a specific purpose or in a specific mode, for example. Used in conjunction with *Elements of Writing*, such a portfolio might contain student responses to the **Chapter Review Writing Prompts** for Chapters 4, 5, 6, 7, 8, 9, and 10.

In addition, the teacher might include one or two evaluations of speeches. Speech Evaluation Forms should prove useful in measuring the student's mastery of oral communication. Some teachers may want to include the results of pretests and mastery tests in grammar, usage, and mechanics.

Teachers who choose this approach usually do not evaluate the portfolio more than two to four times during the academic year. The criteria for assessing the portfolio may vary. Generally, the teacher lists the objectives the portfolio is designed to measure, and then the teacher or some other evaluator decides whether the student has mastered each objective based on the materials in the portfolio. A scale similar to this one may be used to indicate the student's mastery of each objective:

4　The student's work reflects complete mastery of this objective.

3　The student's work indicates acceptable mastery of this objective.

2　The student's work indicates some progress toward mastering this objective.

1　The student has made little or no progress in mastering the objective.

A random sampling of the portfolios should provide reliable data for those interested in using this approach to assess an overall language arts program rather than the progress of individual students.

Portfolio Assessment

The Complete Portfolio. Most teachers find filing every single piece of work each student does burdensome, but some prefer a more detailed picture of a student's work than can be given with the Basic or Mastery portfolios.

In that case, the teacher frequently makes a checklist for each student. The list includes all major assignments for the class and indicates whether the student completed the assignment and how the assignment was evaluated. In addition to the checklist, the portfolio might include a few representative samples of the student's work plus evaluation forms and check sheets for most major assignments, grouped according to the type of assignment. The portfolio may be evaluated in the same way as a Mastery portfolio.

Basic guidelines for portfolio design. Teachers are in the best position to decide what type of portfolio will be most beneficial for their programs and their students. The most important step is to decide what objectives and outcomes the portfolio should assess and then collect materials for the portfolio that will measure the objectives and reflect the outcomes. You may wish to try out some of the model forms supplied in this booklet before duplicating them and introducing them to the students. Ask a few students to use some of the forms Work with each student to determine which records work best in your instruction and whether you want to modify or replace any of them. You may also get ideas for effective ways to introduce each form to the class.

ASSESSMENT MATERIALS

In addition to the guidelines and checklists that appear in the pupil's text, the *Elements of Writing* program includes several components that you may use to assess student work and evaluate progress. These evaluation sheets and checklists, are appropriate for inclusion in student portfolios, but they may be used independently of portfolio assessment.

Assessing Writing. Included in the *Elements of Writing* program are a series of evaluation sheets that offer teachers a variety of options for assessing writing. Teachers who do not choose a holistic approach to assessment may choose from two analytic scales and they may use the forms to allow for peer evaluation or to encourage the student's evaluation of his or her own writing. Those who do choose a holistic approach may use the **Holistically Graded Composition Models** as the basis of their assessment plan.

Assessing Oral Communication and Group Participation. Several forms in the *Elements of Writing* assessment packet are specifically designed to allow teachers and peers to evaluate student speeches, to assess how well a student is listening to an oral presentation, and to assess contributions to group work.

FOR FURTHER READING

Bishop, Wendy, and Crossley, Gay Lynn. (1993) Not only assessment: Teachers talk about writing portfolios. Journal of Teaching Writing, 12 (1), pp. 33–55.
This article shows how using writing portfolio evaluation changes the way that teachers think about their roles, students, and students' writing. (Whole issue is on portfolios.)

Portfolio Assessment

Farr, Roger, and Farr, Beverly. (1990) Language Arts Portfolio Teacher's Manual. Integrated Assessment System. San Antonio: The Psychological Corporation
This manual includes descriptions of how to use, rate, and interpret responses to the Integrated Assessment System and several chapters on developing and using portfolios.

Farr, Roger, and Tone, Bruce. (1994) Portfolio and performance assessment: Helping students evaluate their progress as readers and writers. Fort Worth: Harcourt Brace College Publishers.
Portfolio assessment and the development of performance assessments is explained in detail with numerous practical suggestions, checklists, and model forms. Working portfolios are recommended to promote students' analysis of their own language use.

Galbraith, Marian, et al. (1994) Using portfolios to negotiate a rhetorical community. Report Series 3.10 Albany, New York: National Research Center on Literature Teaching and Learning.
Teaching narration and discussion cover what is required in the negotiation and mentoring involved in becoming a co-assessor with the student of the student's work.

Grady, Emily. (Fall 1992) The portfolio approach to assessment. Fastback Series. Bloomington, Indiana: Phi Delta Kappa.
This booklet tells how to use portfolios to assess a wide range of student performance.

Hewitt, Geof. (1995) A portfolio primer: Teaching, collecting, and assessing student writing. Portsmouth, New Hampshire: Heinemann.
This manual on portfolio assessment covers grades 3–12 and a broad range of key considerations, with generous examples from actual portfolios.

Palmer, Barbara C., et al. (1994) Developing cultural literacy through the writing process: Empowering all learners. Des Moines: Allyn and Bacon.
Emphasizing cultural literacy, this book addresses each stage of the writing process and treats portfolio assessment. Numerous model activities expand the writers knowledge base and develop critical thinking.

Tierney, Robert J.; Carter, Mark A.; and Desai, Laura E. (1991) Portfolio assessment in the reading-writing classroom. Norwood, Massachusetts: Christopher-Gordon.
This presentation covers all aspects of portfolio assessment, relying on research and descriptions of actual implementation.

Valencia, Sheila W., and Place, Nancy. (May 1994) Portfolios: A process for enhancing teaching and learning, The Reading Teacher, 47 (8), pp. 666–669.
Aspects of a Bellevue (Washington) project helped teachers use portfolios effectively.

Valencia, Sheila W. (ed.) et al. (1994) Authentic reading assessment: Practices and possibilities. Newark, Delaware: International Reading Association.
Case studies describe authentic assessment in and beyond the classroom. Programs at particular schools and in particular states are detailed.

Portfolio: Form (1)

Evaluating Your Writing Process

There is no such thing as a single writing process. Every writer and every piece of writing is unique. Choose one paper from your portfolio. Track your writing process for that paper by writing brief answers to these questions. Keep the questions and your answers in your portfolio.

Prewriting

1. How did you decide on your subject?

2. Did you use any of the prewriting techniques we have learned in class? Which ones? How did they work for you with this assignment?

3. Did you plan the organization of your paper before you started writing? Why or why not?

4. What did you like best about this stage of the assignment? What did you like least?

5. About how much time did you spend on this stage of the writing process?

Writing

6. What did you find easiest about writing your draft?

7. What did you find most difficult about writing your draft?

8. What was your primary concern while writing the draft? Organization? Style? Development? Something else? Why?

9. What did you like best about this stage of the writing process? What did you like least?

10. About how much time did you spend writing your draft?

Evaluating and Revising

11. Did you receive feedback on your draft from anyone? If so, was the feedback helpful? Why or why not?

12. What did you think about your draft? Why?

13. Did you make major changes in your draft? Why or why not?

14. What did you like best about this stage of the writing process? What did you like least?

15. About how much time did you spend evaluating and revising your draft?

Proofreading and Publishing

16. How did you go about proofreading your paper?

17. How would you describe the final appearance of the paper?

18. Where did you publish your paper?

19. What did you like best about this stage of the writing process? What did you like least?

20. About how much time did you devote to proofreading and preparing your paper for publication?

Portfolio: Form (2)

Creating a Guide for Evaluating Papers

Check off each step as the class completes the activity.

_____ 1. The students read their papers aloud. No one comments until everyone has read.

_____ 2. The class chooses two or three papers that they especially like.

_____ 3. The students decide what the papers have in common that makes them good.

_____ 4. The students list the four most important criteria in the form of complete sentences. Each sentence begins "A good paper has (or does) . . . ."

_____ 5. The students review the writing assignment to decide if they want to include additional criteria, and any new criteria are added to the list.

_____ 6. Working independently, in pairs, or in peer groups, the students evaluate their papers using the criteria as a guide, indicating how successful their papers have been in achieving each goal. (1 = Not at all successful, 2 = Somewhat successful, 3 = Almost totally successful, 4 = Totally successful)

As a final step, students might meet in small groups to ask peer advice on how to rewrite in order to achieve a four (4) on all criteria.

Portfolio: Form (3)

Revising Your Draft

Read through your rough draft using the following five steps as a guide. Answer each question fully and thoughtfully. Check off each step as you complete it.

_____ **Step 1—Thinking About Your Readers**

State how you want your readers to react to your paper.

_____

_____

_____

Read through your paper quickly without stopping. Then state what you think the readers' reactions will be.

_____

_____

_____

If the readers' reactions are likely to be different than the reaction you want, what do you need to change in the paper?

_____

_____

_____

_____ **Step 2—Looking at Your Introduction**

Look closely at the introduction to your paper. What does the introduction do to capture the readers' interest?

_____

_____

_____

What do you like best about your introduction? _____

_____

What do you like least? _____

_____

What might you add, cut, replace, or reorder to strengthen your introduction?

_____

_____

_____

Portfolio: Form (3)

Revising Your Draft

_____ **Step 3—Looking at the Body**

Read carefully through the body of your paper. What main points or ideas do you want your readers to understand?

_____

_____

_____

_____

Do you think the reader will consider the order of your ideas or points logical? _____

Explain. _____

_____

_____

What examples of specific language do you find in the body of the essay? _____

_____

_____

Does this assignment call for examples and facts? _____ If so, what examples and facts have you used?

_____

_____

_____

Where might additional facts and examples be helpful?

_____

_____

_____

Do any facts or examples seem unrelated or unnecessary?

_____

_____

_____

What might you add, cut, replace, or reorder to strengthen the body of the paper?

_____

_____

_____

Portfolio: Form (3)

Revising Your Draft

_____ **Step 4—Looking at the Conclusion**

Look closely at the conclusion to your paper. What does the conclusion do to bring the paper to a satisfactory close?

_____

_____

_____

What do you like best about your conclusion? _____

_____

What do you like least? _____

_____

What might you add, cut, replace, or reorder to strengthen your conclusion? _____

_____

_____ **Step 5—Hearing How the Paper Sounds**

Read your paper aloud. Which sentences sound especially good to you?

_____

_____

_____

Which sentences seem awkward, wordy, or unclear? _____

_____

_____

_____

What words or phrases might you add, cut, replace, or reorder to strengthen those sentences?

_____

_____

_____

_____

_____

Portfolio: Form (4)

Revision Checklist

Revise your paper until you can answer yes to each of the following questions. Add, cut, replace, or reorder material in your paper as necessary.

	Yes	No
Content		
1. Does the paper have a clear introduction?		
2. Is the body of the paper well developed?		
3. Does the paper end in a way that is satisfying to a reader?		
4. Are the subject and purpose of the paper clear?		
5. Does the paper achieve its purpose?		
6. Is each main idea in the paper developed with facts or details?		
7. Is the paper free of unrelated or unnecessary ideas?		
8. Is the paper interesting?		
Organization		
9. Are the ideas and details arranged in a clear order?		
10. Have transitions been used to make clear the relationships between sentences and paragraphs?		
Style		
11. Is every sentence in the paper clear?		
12. Is the language of the paper appropriate for its audience and purpose?		
13. Have you avoided stringy and wordy sentences? Have you varied your sentence length and type?		

Portfolio: Form (5)

Evaluating a Paper

Writer's Name _____

Title of Paper _____

Introduction

The best thing about the introduction is _____

_____

_____

To improve the introduction, the writer might _____

_____

_____

Body

The two best things about the body are _____

_____

_____

To improve the body, the writer might _____

_____

_____

Conclusion

The best thing about the conclusion is _____

_____

_____

To improve the conclusion, the writer might _____

_____

_____

Overall Evaluation

What does this writer do best of all? _____

_____

_____

Circle the element that the writer should concentrate on most when revising.

Interest Level   Style   Organization   Development

Portfolio: Form (6)

Evaluating a Paper

1. Which part of the writing did you find most interesting? Why? _____
   _____
   _____

2. Which part of the writing might the writer make more interesting? _____
   _____
   _____

   How would you suggest that the writer do this? _____
   _____
   _____

3. What is the writer's purpose? How can you tell? _____
   _____
   _____

   Do you think the writer is successful in achieving the purpose? Explain. _____
   _____
   _____

4. Are any parts of the paper difficult to read or understand?
   If so, which ones and why? _____
   _____
   _____

5. How would you characterize the writer's ability to edit and proofread?
   Explain. _____
   _____
   _____

6. When the writer revises, is there anything that he or she definitely should not change? ____
   _____
   _____

7. Tell the writer two specific things to do to improve the paper. _____
   _____
   _____

Portfolio: Form (7)

Analytic Scale for Evaluation

The **Points Possible** for each of the twelve criteria listed in the chart may vary depending on the writing assignment that is being evaluated. Your teacher may give you the points possible for each category. Or, for some assignments, your teacher may give you the responsibility of deciding the points possible. After you have filled the **Points Possible** column, read the paper (your own or a classmate's) carefully and thoughtfully. Complete the **Points Given** column and tally the score.

Content	Points Possible	Points Given
1. Is the writing interesting?		
2. Does the writing achieve its purpose?		
3. Are there enough details?		
4. Are the ideas related to the topic?		
Organization		
5. Are ideas and details arranged in an effective order?		
6. Are the connections between ideas clear?		
Style		
7. Is the meaning of each sentence clear?		
8. Does the language fit the audience and purpose?		
9. Do sentences read smoothly?		
Grammar and Usage		
10. Is the paper relatively free of problems in grammar and usage?		
Punctuation and Capitalization		
11. Is the paper relatively free of problems in punctuation and capitalization?		
Spelling and Manuscript Form		
12. Is the paper relatively free of problems in spelling and manuscript form?		
Total Points		

Portfolio: Form (8)

Simplified Analytic Scales

	Points Possible	Points Given
Content	20	
Organization	20	
Style	20	
Grammar and Usage	20	
Spelling, Mechanics, and Manuscript Form	20	
Total	100	

	Points Possible	Points Given
Content	25	
Organization	25	
Style	25	
Spelling, Grammar, Usage, and Mechanics	25	
Total	100	

Name _____ Date _____ Class _____

Self-assessment Record

Rating: Needs improvement   Satisfactory   Outstanding
                 1   2   3   4   5

Title or Description of Paper or Product	What you like:	What you don't like:	Rating

Portfolio: Form (9)

Peer Evaluation Form

Directions for evaluators: Read the following list of criteria for good writing. Then, with these criteria in mind, read your classmate's paper. Finally, based on the criteria, rank the piece of writing from **1** to **4**, with **1** being the lowest ranking and **4** being the highest. Be ready to discuss your evaluation with the writer and to make suggestions for revising the paper.

Criteria for Evaluation:

1. The writing is interesting.

2. The writing achieves its purpose.

3. The writing contains enough details.

4. The writing does not contain unrelated ideas.

5. The ideas and details are arranged in an effective order.

6. The connections between ideas and between sentences are clear.

7. The writer's meaning is clear throughout.

8. The language fits the audience and purpose of the piece of writing.

9. The sentences read smoothly.

10. The paper is free (or almost free) of problems in grammar and usage.

11. The paper is free (or almost free) of problems in punctuation and capitalization.

12. The paper is free (or almost free) of problems in spelling and manuscript form.

Ranking _____

Name _____ Date _____ Class _____

Peer Evaluation Form

Writer's Name _____

Title of Paper _____

---

1. The most effective sentence in this paper is_____
   _____
   _____

2. The most effective words or phrases in this paper are _____
   _____
   _____
   _____

3. The most interesting idea in this paper is _____
   _____
   _____

4. The part of this paper that I will remember best is_____
   _____
   _____
   _____

Signed _____

Peer Evaluator

Portfolio: Form (11)

Proofreading Checklist

Proofread your paper using each of the following steps. Put a check by each step after you complete it.

_____ 1. Read the paper backward word by word.

_____ 2. Make a large card with a word-size hole in it and move it over the page.

_____ 3. Read the first sentence in your paper carefully. Put your left index finger on the punctuation mark that signals the end of that sentence. Now put your right index finger on the punctuation mark that ends the second sentence. Carefully read the material between your fingers; then move your left index finger to the end of the second sentence and your right to the end of the third, and read carefully. Keep moving your fingers until you have carefully examined each sentence in the paper.

List the mistakes you discovered when proofreading.

_____

_____

_____

_____

_____

_____

_____

_____

_____

_____

_____

_____

_____

_____

_____

_____

_____

_____

Portfolio: Form (12)

Proofreading Checklist

Read through the paper and then mark the following statements either **T** for true or **F** for false. Return the paper and the checklist to the writer. Give the writer time to locate and correct the errors. After the writer has done the best he or she can to correct the paper, offer to assist if your help is needed.

_____ 1. The paper is neat.

_____ 2. Each sentence begins with a capital letter.

_____ 3. Each sentence ends with a period, question mark, or exclamation mark.

_____ 4. Each sentence is complete. Each has a subject and a predicate and expresses a complete thought.

_____ 5. A singular verb is used with each singular subject, and a plural verb with each plural subject.

_____ 6. Nominative case pronouns such as *I* and *we* are used for subjects; objective case pronouns such as *me* and *us* are used for objects.

_____ 7. Singular pronouns are used to refer to singular nouns, and plural pronouns are used to refer to plural nouns.

_____ 8. Each word is spelled correctly.

_____ 9. Frequently confused verbs, such as *lie/lay*, *sit/set*, and *rise/raise* are used correctly.

_____ 10. Other frequently confused words, such as *all ready/already*, *farther/further*, and *fewer/less* are used correctly.

_____ 11. Double negatives are avoided.

_____ 12. All proper nouns and proper adjectives are capitalized.

_____ 13. Word endings such as *–s*, *–ing*, and *–ed* are included where they should be.

_____ 14. No words have been accidentally left out.

_____ 15. No words have been accidentally written twice.

_____ 16. Each paragraph is indented.

_____ 17. Apostrophes are used correctly with contractions and possessive nouns.

_____ 18. Dialogue is punctuated and capitalized correctly.

_____ 19. Any correction that could not be rewritten or retyped is crossed out with a single line.

Name _____ Date _____ Class _____

Proofreading Record

Keeping a record of your mistakes can be helpful. For the next few writing assignments, list the errors your teacher or your peers find in your work. If you faithfully use this kind of record, you'll find it easier to avoid troublesome errors.

Errors and Corrections for Writing Assignment # _____

Title _____ Date _____

Write sentences that contain errors in grammar or usage here.
_____
_____
_____
_____
_____
_____
_____
_____

Write corrections here.
_____
_____
_____
_____
_____
_____
_____

Write sentences that contain errors in mechanics here.
_____
_____
_____
_____
_____
_____
_____
_____

Write corrections here.
_____
_____
_____
_____
_____
_____
_____

Write misspelled words here.
_____
_____
_____
_____
_____
_____
_____
_____

Write corrections here.
_____
_____
_____
_____
_____
_____
_____

Proofreading Record

	Title or Description of Assignment									
Directions: When your teacher returns a corrected writing assignment, write the topic in the appropriate box. Under the topic, record the number of errors you made in each area. Use this sheet when you proofread your next assignment, taking care to check those areas in which you make frequent mistakes.										
ERROR										
Sentence Fragments										
Run-on Sentences										
Subject-Verb Agreement										
Pronoun Agreement										
Incorrect Pronoun Form										
Use of Double Negative										
Comparison of Adjectives and Adverbs										
Confusing Verbs										
Irregular Verbs										
Noun Plurals and Possessives										
Capitalization										
Spelling Rules										
End Punctuation										
Apostrophe										
Confusing Words										
Quotation Marks and Italics										
Comma or Paired Commas										

Portfolio: Form (16)

Spelling Log

Correctly spelled word:	How I misspelled it:	What part I misspelled:	How I can remember the correct spelling:

Portfolio: Form (17)

Inventory of Reading and Writing

What three words best describe you as a reader?

_____

Explain why you think these words are true of you.

_____

_____

_____

What types of reading material do you like best (magazines, novels, poetry, short stories, nonfiction, etc.)? What topics do you like best to read about (adventure, mystery, war, romance, etc.)?

_____

_____

_____

What are the titles of some specific things that you have read recently?

_____

_____

Make an *x* where you would place yourself on the scale below:

   I read very little   I don't read very much   I read quite a bit   I read a lot
----

What three words best describe you as a writer?

_____

Explain why you think these words are true of you.

_____

_____

_____

What type of writing do you like best (writing stories, writing journals, writing letters, writing poetry, etc.)? What topics do you like best to write about (fantasy, real life, memories, ideas, etc.)?

_____

_____

_____

Name _____ Date _____ Class _____

Inventory of Reading and Writing

Make an *x* where you would place yourself on the scale below:

I write very little   I don't write very much   I write quite a bit   I write a lot

- -

What are your biggest problems as a reader?

_____

_____

_____

What ideas do you have about dealing with these problems?

_____

_____

_____

What are your biggest problems as a as a writer?

_____

_____

_____

What ideas do you have about dealing with these problems?

_____

_____

_____

Teacher's comments:

Name _____ Date _____ Class _____

Reading Record

Ratings:	I didn't like it	Not bad	OK	Very Good	Terrific
	○	☆	☆☆	☆☆☆	☆☆☆☆

Month / Day	Title and Author	Rating	Free response: What do you remember? What did you like?

Month / Day	Teacher's Comments

Name _____ Date _____ Class _____

Progress in Reading: Teacher's Report

Volume of Reading	Rating Scale and Comments
Compared with classmates	Needs improvement Satisfactory Excellent 1.................2.................3.............4.................5 Comments: _____
Compared with last progress report:	Needs improvement Satisfactory Excellent 1.................2.................3.............4.................5 Comments: _____
Amount the student is reading during the designated time in class	Needs improvement Satisfactory Excellent 1.................2.................3.............4.................5 Comments: _____
Amount the student is reading outside of class:	Needs improvement Satisfactory Excellent 1.................2.................3.............4.................5 Comments: _____
Reading Interests	
Student is able to choose reading material of personal interest	Needs improvement Satisfactory Excellent 1.................2.................3.............4.................5 Comments: _____
Student is willing to explore new topics:	Needs improvement Satisfactory Excellent 1.................2.................3.............4.................5 Comments: _____
Student is willing to talk about reading with teacher and other students:	Needs improvement Satisfactory Excellent 1.................2.................3.............4.................5 Comments: _____
Attitude about Reading	
Student is willing to reading attentively during designated in-class reading time	Needs improvement Satisfactory Excellent 1.................2.................3.............4.................5 Comments: _____

Name _____ Date _____ Class _____

Progress in Reading: Teacher's Report

Attitude about Reading	
Student is responsible in bringing appropriate reading material to class for in-class reading:	Needs improvement Satisfactory Excellent 1.................2.................3.................4.................5 Comments: _____
Student keeps up with portfolio assessment of reading; is reflective about progress as a reader:	Needs improvement Satisfactory Excellent 1.................2.................3.................4.................5 Comments: _____
Applied Comprehension	
Student is able to respond to reading in writing and speaking:	Needs improvement Satisfactory Excellent 1.................2.................3.................4.................5 Comments: _____
Student is able to relate reading to life experience in speaking and writing	Needs improvement Satisfactory Excellent 1.................2.................3.................4.................5 Comments: _____
Reading Strategies	
Asks questions about reading problems:	Needs improvement Satisfactory Excellent 1.................2.................3.................4.................5 Comments: _____
Has strategies to deal with reading problems in comprehension and vocabulary	Needs improvement Satisfactory Excellent 1.................2.................3.................4.................5 Comments: _____

Additional Comments

Name _____ Date _____ Class _____

Speaking and Listening-Viewing Record

Ratings: I didn't like it   Not bad   OK   Very Good   Terrific

☆   ☆☆   ☆☆☆   ☆☆☆☆

Month / Day	Title or Description of Activity	Free response: What do you remember? What did you like?	Rating

	Teacher's comments

Portfolio: Form (21)

Inventory of Speaking, Listening, and Viewing

When is talking the most fun for you? With whom? About what?

When is talking difficult? In what situations? About what topics?

When is it easiest for you to talk in class? When do you feel most comfortable about classroom talk?

When is talking in class difficult or uncomfortable for you?

When is it easiest for you to listen attentively? To whom? About what?

Portfolio: Form (21, cont.)

Inventory of Speaking, Listening, and Viewing

When is watching videos or performances attentively the easiest for you?

When is it hard to listen or watch attentively? Why is it hard?

What strategies do you know to help you critically evaluate what you view?

Teacher's Comments

Portfolio: Form (22)

Evaluating an Oral Book Report

Circle 1, 2, or 3 to indicate how well the speaker met the following criteria.

1 = Not at all   2 = To some extent   3 = Successfully

1. The speaker mentioned the author and title of the book early in the speech.	1	2	3
2. The speaker's attitude toward the book was clear early in the presentation.	1	2	3
3. The speaker supported his or her opinions with evidence from the book.	1	2	3
4. The evidence was clearly organized and presented.	1	2	3
5. The speaker did not merely summarize the book.	1	2	3
6. The report made it clear that the speaker has read the book critically and closely.	1	2	3
7. The speaker's report was interesting to the audience.	1	2	3
8. The speaker's voice was clear and distinct.	1	2	3
9. The speaker maintained eye contact with the audience.	1	2	3
10. The speaker used good body language.	1	2	3

Portfolio: Form (23)

Evaluating a Speech

Aspect of Speech	Evaluation
Introduction	
Body	
Conclusion	
Word Choice	
Verbal Communication	
Nonverbal Communication	

Name _____ Date _____ Class _____

Peer Evaluation Form for Speech

Speaker _____ Speech Topic _____

To evaluate a speech, place an **X** in the appropriate box following each item.

CONTENT	Very Good	Good	Poor
Interesting introduction			
Clear statement of the main idea			
Selection of supporting ideas			
Clear organization of ideas			
Conclusion			
Effective use of language			
Effective visual aids			
DELIVERY			
Eye contact			
Volume			
Pronunciation and expression			
Gestures			
Poise and self-control			

COMMENTS: What I liked most about your speech was _____

_____

_____

_____

_____

If you could improve one element of your speech, I would suggest that you try to _____

_____

_____

_____

_____

Portfolio: Form (25)

Evaluating Critical Listening

To evaluate your ability to listen critically, answer the following questions about an oral presentation you recently heard. Compare your answers with those of other classmates who also heard the presentation.

If you can't answer any of the questions, explain why.

1. What was the speaker's purpose? _____

_____

_____

2. What main points did the speaker make? _____

_____

_____

3. What examples, details, illustrations, or facts do you remember from the

presentation? _____

_____

_____

4. Explain why you think the speaker chose to use the materials you listed in your

answer to Question 3. Be specific about as many items as you can. _____

_____

_____

5. What did the speaker say that puzzled or bothered you? How did that affect how

you reacted to the presentation? _____

_____

_____

_____

6. What did you consider to be the strengths of the presentation? _____

_____

_____

7. Did you note any weaknesses? If so, what were they? _____

_____

_____

_____

Name _____ Date _____ Class _____

Evaluating Group Participation

You may use this form to evaluate the contributions of another student in the group.

The group member I am evaluating is _____ .

The group member's role in the group was _____ .

The word I would use to describe how the group member performed the role is

_____ .

The most important contribution the member made to the group was

_____

_____

_____ .

The group member could contribute more to the group if he or she

_____

_____

_____ .

Portfolio: Form (27)

Evaluating Group Participation

Use this form as a guide to thinking about your contribution to group activities.

1. What was your role in the group today? _____

_____

_____

2. What did you need to do to be useful in that role? _____

_____

_____

_____

3. What was your most important contribution to the group today? _____

_____

_____

_____

_____

4. What could you do to become a more effective group member? _____

_____

_____

_____

_____

Name _____ Date _____ Class _____

Evaluating Group Participation

Think about the work your small group did today and then answer the following questions.

The students who participated in this group were _____

_____.

Our task was _____.

Circle your response to the following statements.

1 = Strongly Disagree   2 = Disagree Somewhat   3 = Agree   4 = Strongly Agree

The group did a good job of staying on task.	1	2	3	4
Every member of the group contributed something to the group.	1	2	3	4
Each member of the group treated the other members of the group with respect and kindness.	1	2	3	4
The group felt that the task was worth accomplishing.	1	2	3	4
Each member of the group learned something from this experience.	1	2	3	4

What is the group's greatest strength? _____

_____.

What does this group need to do to become more productive? _____

_____

_____.

Name _____ Date _____ Class _____

Summary of Progress

Grade _____ School year _____ I started this portfolio on _____

In which areas of language use have you made an effort to improve (either in quantity or quality) since the last evaluation? Circle all that apply.	What specific progress have you made in the areas you circled?
Reading quantity Reading quality Writing quantity Writing quality Speaking quantity Speaking quality Listening quantity Listening quality	Reading: Writing: Speaking: Listening:
What improvements would you like to make in any of these areas between now and the next evaluation?	At the present time, which areas are you strongest in? What are your strengths in these areas?
Reading: Writing: Speaking: Listening:	Reading: Writing: Speaking: Listening:
At the present time, which areas are you weakest in? What are your weaknesses in these areas?	Which pieces in your portfolio are examples of your best? Which pieces need more work?
Reading: Writing: Speaking: Listening:	The best: Need more work:

Ask your teacher or another student to write comments about your portfolio on the back side of this form.

Name _____ Date _____ Class _____

Description of Portfolio Contents

Grade _____ School year _____ I started this portfolio on _____

Explain the system of organization you used to arrange your portfolio.

General Comments
After reviewing the work in your portfolio, what generalizations can you make about yourself as a reader?
After reviewing the work in your portfolio, what generalizations can you make about yourself as a writer?
After reviewing the work in your portfolio, what generalizations can you make about yourself as a speaker and listener?

Special Notice	
Choose two texts that you think are the best things you have read for this portfolio and comment briefly on why you liked them.	Title: Comment: Title: Comment:
Choose two texts that you think are the best things you have written for this portfolio and comment briefly on why you think these are the best.	Title: Comment: Title: Comment:
What other pieces in your portfolio would you like someone looking at your portfolio to notice? What do these pieces show about the way you are able to use language?	Title: Comment: Title: Comment:

Name _____ Date _____ Class _____

Progress Report: Student Awareness of Language as Process

Ratings:	Minimal progress 1	2	Satisfactory progress 3	4	Outstanding progress 5

Process Strategy	Rating	Comment
Uses language with a conscious purpose: Can articulate purposes which motivate his or her reading, writing, listening, and speaking activities.		
Uses prior knowledge to guide language use. Demonstrates that he or she makes use of what is already known before and during an activity language use.		
Anticipates what can be learned or confirmed in using language. Can articulate the implications of clues prior to language use; preplans expression.		
Makes predictions in using language. Can articulate predictions in text and oral presentations and can articulate audience expectations.		
Visualizes meaning. Can articulate visualizations of the meaning being made by reading, writing, listening, and speaking as the process proceeds.		
Challenges meaning. Can articulate questions about the cogency and appropriateness of the ideas, concepts, and details presented.		
Adjusts language strategies. Articulates possible strategy adjustments needed in order to construct clear meaning.		
Seeks aid or advice. Will ask for help when strategies do not resolve inability to construct clear meaning.		

Name _____ Date _____ Class _____

Progress Report: Graph of Student's Performance as a Language User Across Time Periods

Key Considerations in Growth of Language Use. Place the appropriate symbol for each category opposite the rating for each period. Connect the symbols with different colored lines to create a chart.

● Attitude toward using language. *How much does student enjoy reading, writing, speaking, and listening?*

☆ Involvement in improvement. *How inclined is student to self-assess, revise, and set new language use goals?*

✕ Amount/frequency of use. *How often does the student read, write, and speak with a clear purpose?*

✓ Effectiveness of use. *How strong is student's control of language conventions, diction, and style?*

Ratings:

10 = Outstanding performance

8 = Good performance

6⎫
4⎬= Satisfactory performance

2 = Weak performance

Rating	1st Period	2nd Period	3rd Period	4th Period	Comments: How much overall progress has this student shown?
10					
9					
8					
7					
6					
5					
4					
3					
2					
1					

Teacher _____

School year _____

Name _____ Date _____ Class _____

Your Student's Portfolio: What it Shows About Your Student's Use of Language

In the left column of the chart below I have noted several aspects of this portfolio that I believe to be especially important in assessing your student's use of language. In the right column I have commented on your student's progress in each of these aspects.

The portfolio includes papers that your student has collected over a period of time. In it you will see various types of writing, reactions to reading, and evidence of other language use. Many of the writings are accompanied by earlier drafts that show how the work has evolved from a raw idea to a finished piece of writing. Besides collecting these papers and keeping logs on how he or she uses language, your student is responsible for organizing and analyzing the papers in the portfolio. The material in the portfolio therefore demonstrates two of the primary goals of portfolio-keeping: teaching the student that using language is a process, and developing the student's habit of analyzing and evaluating his or her own work.

Aspects of this portfolio that I believe are significant:	What these aspects of the portfolio demonstrate about your student's use of language:

Teacher's signature: _____

Name _____ Date _____ Class _____

Response to the Portfolio

Please answer any questions that seem important to you. You can also write comments on the reverse side.

Parent or Guardian _____ Date _____

What does this portfolio tell you about your student's progress in reading?

_____

_____

What does this portfolio tell you about your student's progress in writing?

_____

_____

What surprised you about your student's portfolio? Why was this surprising?

_____

_____

What are the three or four pieces in your student's portfolio that especially impressed you? Why did these pieces impress you?

_____

_____

_____

_____

What did you like best about your student's portfolio? Why did you like this best?

_____

_____

What questions do you have about your student's portfolio?

_____

_____

What would you like to see the next time you look at your student's portfolio?

_____

_____